The Neglected Wisdom

Uncovering What Shapes Your Destiny

Chuks Eze

The views expressed in this work are solely those of the author and do not necessarily reflect the views of the publisher, and the publisher hereby disclaims any responsibility for them.

First edition

ISBN: 978-1-917293-31-0

Dedication

This book is dedicated to each of you, with heartfelt gratitude for the love, support, and encouragement that have shaped this journey. May our bond continue to be strengthened.

To my beloved parents, Mr. Jonathan and Felicity Eze, whose wisdom has been a guiding light in my life. From the earliest days of my childhood to my adulthood, your words of wisdom have shaped some of my decisions.

To my cherished wife, Lovelyn, thank you for believing in me, supporting me, and giving me the midnight hours at the study desk to write this book.

And to our dear children, Joyce and Joshua, whose boundless enthusiasm and encouragement have fuelled my determination to see this project through to completion. Thank you for that enthusiastic support.

Contents

Acknowledgments

I would like to express my profound gratitude to Professor Dilly Anumba, MBBS, FWACS, MD, MRCOG, LLM Medical Law, who graciously agreed to write the Foreword for this book. Professor Anumba, a distinguished expert in Obstetrics and Gynaecology at the University of Sheffield and Consultant in Maternal and Fetal Medicine at Sheffield Teaching Hospitals NHS Foundation Trust, has shown unwavering support for this project.

I also want to acknowledge my friends, whose wise counsel and encouragement have shaped my path and guided me in the right direction. Thank you, Jonathan Dzakpata, for your invaluable assistance with the book cover design review. Your feedback greatly enhanced the final product.

Lastly, I wish to recognise the men and women of great influence whose teachings have had a positive impact on me. Figures like the late Napoleon Hill, Oprah Winfrey,

Dr. David Oyedepo, the late Earl Nightingale, Dr Ngozi Okonjo-Iweala, and the late Bob Proctor have inspired me through their words and works, enriching my life and perspective.

Foreword

Many books reflect on how best to navigate the challenges and exigencies of life. Some are biographies, while others address principles and ideals of successful living. However, few illustrate and tease out how to embed wisdom—the effective application of knowledge—in a relatable way to a wide readership.

In this book, Chuks Eze deftly achieves this by sharing his knowledge and experiences across the entire spectrum of life and living: growing up, being a parent, being a spouse, relating with the wider family and people in our spheres of influence, and applying wisdom to address all of life's challenges. There is a poignant exposition of how wisdom can mandate personal sacrifices and delayed gratification, aiming for future success and more auspicious rewards. Chuks reveals the innate, often neglected, wisdom in people, which, if recognized and harnessed, can empower individuals to achieve success and destiny. I particularly relate to the nuggets of wisdom he espouses regarding self-belief.

I enthusiastically commend Chuks's excellent exposition of wisdom in this book to all. The subject is approached from unique yet practical perspectives. It is a compelling, easy read that unravels and explains its subjects very nicely.

It should not only be read but also gifted to and shared with people in our lives.

Professor Dilly OC Anumba,

MBBS FWACS FRCOG MD LL.M (Medical Law)

Chair of Obstetrics and Gynaecology

Honorary Consultant Obstetrician/Gynaecologist,

Subspecialist in Maternal and Fetal Medicine

Honorary Professor, University of Cape Town, South Africa

Director, NIHR Global Health Research Group on Preterm Birth,

Introduction

Wisdom is the compass that guides us through the labyrinth of life. It illuminates our path, enabling us to make choices that shape our destiny. Every day, wisdom calls out to us, seeking our attention with the fervour of a suitor pursuing their beloved. Its voice resonates through the chaos of our lives, offering insights and warnings to steer us away from danger.

Like a precious jewel hidden in the depths of the earth, wisdom awaits those who are willing to seek it diligently. It does not hide itself from those who earnestly desire its guidance; rather, it eagerly opens its doors to those who knock, inviting them to partake in its riches.

The question that echoes through the corridors of time is this: Are you willing to embark on the quest for wisdom? Are you ready to unearth its treasures and apply its teachings to every facet of your existence? The journey of wisdom is not for the faint of heart, but for those who dare to tread its path, the rewards are boundless.

As you set out on this journey, consider the legacy you wish to leave behind. Legacy is not measured by material wealth or social status, but by the impact we have on those around us. Whether in the realm of family, career, or education, each of us has the power to shape the legacy we leave for future generations.

Our journey begins with the miracle of birth, a testament to the resilience of the human spirit and the boundless capacity for love. From the anticipation of pregnancy to the sleepless nights of parenthood, we navigate the joys and challenges of raising a child. Along the way, we confront choices that shape the course of our lives, from the method of feeding to the financial implications of childcare.

In the sanctuary of the family, we discover the true meaning of love and belonging. Amidst the complexities of relationships, we learn to navigate the intricacies of human connection with grace and understanding. Siblings bond, relatives unite, and through it all, we find strength in the ties that bind us together.

As individuals, we are each imbued with a unique essence—a spark of divinity that sets us apart from all others. Our journey of growth and self-discovery is a testament to the beauty of our individuality and the boundless potential that resides within each of us.

While education and career act as vehicles for our personal and professional growth, enabling us to chase our passions and fulfil our aspirations, genuine success transcends mere worldly accomplishments. It resides in nurturing the virtues listed in the subsection of this book - 'Virtue: A Wise Word That Is Seldom Used'.

Throughout our journey, we draw inspiration from those who have come before us, defying the odds and transcending the limitations imposed by society. In moments of adversity, we find strength in our resilience and courage in our vulnerability.

As we navigate the ever-changing landscape of life, we embrace the inevitability of change, recognising that our ability to adapt and evolve is the key to our survival. And in the face of death, we find solace in the knowledge that our legacy will endure, guiding future generations on their own journey of discovery.

So, dear reader, fasten your seatbelt and join me as we embark on this voyage of self-discovery and enlightenment. May you emerge from these pages blessed with wisdom and inspired to embrace the legacy that awaits you. Enjoy the journey, for it is in the journey itself that we find meaning and purpose.

Caveat: This is not an exhaustive list of wisdom, however, practicing the principles listed and wisdom tips described in this book can significantly shape and improve your life.

Chapter One

The beginning of the journey

Every journey in life has a distinct beginning and end, much like the journey of pregnancy. Just as planning a holiday involves careful consideration and preparation, so too does the journey of bringing a new life into the world. From the moment of conception, a series of decisions and actions are set into motion, akin to booking a holiday.

The process of pregnancy involves myriad activities and experiences, much like preparing for a trip abroad. There are decisions to be made regarding prenatal care, choosing the country, city, and hospital for the birth, and making arrangements for the baby's arrival. Just as packing luggage is essential for travel, expectant parents must prepare for the arrival of their newborn by gathering essentials such as clothing, diapers, and nursery items.

As the pregnancy progresses, anticipation builds, much like the excitement of traveling to a new destination. The journey to the hospital or birthing centre becomes a pivotal moment, akin to the journey to the airport. It is a time filled with anticipation, nerves, and a sense of wonder at the journey ahead.

The experience of childbirth itself can be likened to the experience of take-off and landing during a flight. It is a moment of intense emotion, filled with both exhilaration and trepidation. And just as the quiet moments inside the cabin before take-off can be reflective and serene, so too are the moments of anticipation before the arrival of a new life.

While the journey of pregnancy and childbirth may vary for each individual, it is undeniably a profound and transformative experience. It marks the beginning of a new chapter in life, filled with joy, challenges, and the promise of new beginnings.

Before the miracle of birth, there may be moments of pain and discomfort, but the joy of holding your newborn in your arms makes it all worthwhile. And so, the journey of pregnancy, with all its twists and turns, remains one of life's most remarkable experiences.

In recognising the profound significance of this journey, it is essential for expectant parents to approach it with wisdom and mindfulness. Just as they prepare for the practical aspects of childbirth, they must also cultivate an awareness of their responsibilities to the life they are bringing into the world. By embracing this journey with intentionality and grace, they set the stage for a future filled with love, joy, and boundless possibilities.

Raising the child or children

Bringing up children is undeniably one of life's most profound experiences. It's a journey marked by moments of boundless joy, coupled with challenges that test our patience and resilience. However, amidst the laughter and tears, it's essential to recognise that parenthood is a privilege not everyone shares, and those without children should never feel any less blessed.

For my wife and I, the arrival of our firstborn brought with it a cascade of sleepless nights that left us stumbling through our days exhausted. We found ourselves taking shifts during the night; I would be in the lounge, wide awake with our daughter, while my wife caught a few precious hours of sleep, and vice versa. We were initially committed to the idea of exclusive breastfeeding, but our daughter's constant need for nourishment left us feeling overwhelmed and exhausted. It became clear that we needed to adapt our approach. When our second child entered the world, we embraced a combination of breastfeeding and bottle feeding. This adjustment allowed both our baby and us to get the rest we so desperately needed. Gone were the days of stumbling through the fog of exhaustion; instead, we were able to wake up refreshed, ready to check on our little one and face the day with renewed energy and clarity.

From the moment a child is born, a new chapter begins, filled with countless moments of wonder and love. The first time they grasp your finger, their infectious laughter, and the pride in their eyes as they achieve milestones – these are the moments that make parenthood truly special.

Watching your child grow and flourish, witnessing their curiosity and imagination, and sharing in their triumphs and achievements are unparalleled joys. The bond forged between parent and child is a treasure beyond measure, enriching our lives in ways we never thought possible.

However, parenthood also comes with its fair share of challenges. The sleepless nights, the tantrums, and the constant juggling of responsibilities can be overwhelming at times. Every decision, from choosing the right school to navigating disciplinary issues, comes with its own set of uncertainties. So when your child starts to throw some attitude that isn't anticipated or in your vison board, just stay calm, assertive in your words and maintain your set values with great love without compromising it.

Balancing work and family life, maintaining a harmonious household, and providing for your children's emotional and financial needs require unwavering dedication and sacrifice. It's a constant learning curve, filled with moments of self-doubt and exhaustion. As a father, I am constantly learning, unlearning, and juggling various roles to ensure my family continues to move forward and thrive.

Acknowledging Different Paths

While raising children brings immeasurable joy to many, it's essential to acknowledge that not everyone's journey leads to parenthood. Some may struggle with infertility, while others may choose a different path in life. Whatever the reason, not having children should not diminish one's worth or happiness.

Every individual's journey is unique, and fulfilment can be found in different ways – through meaningful relationships, fulfilling careers, or pursuing passions and hobbies. Parenthood is just one chapter in the book of life, and there are countless other avenues to explore and enjoy.

Celebrating Diversity

In celebrating the joys of parenthood, we must also embrace diversity and inclusivity. Families come in all shapes and sizes, and love knows no bounds. Whether through biological children, adoption, or fostering, the love and care provided by parents are what truly matter.

Moreover, let us extend compassion and support to those who may be struggling with infertility or the loss of a child. Their journey may be marked by pain and heartache, but they are no less deserving of love and understanding.

Raising children is a journey filled with both joys and challenges, shaping us into better, more compassionate individuals along the way. However, let us also recognise that parenthood is not the only path to fulfilment, and those without children should never feel any less blessed.

Flexible and Understanding

Be flexible and Consider flexibility as a cornerstone of wisdom, an indispensable quality that allows us to navigate life's twists and turns with grace and resilience. Flexibility entails being open to adjusting our plans and expectations in response to both expected and unexpected circumstances.

Imagine planning to have a family with five children, envisioning a mix of boys and girls. However, as life unfolds, you find yourself in a different reality where you can only afford to raise three children, all girls. In such a situation, flexibility means embracing this change wholeheartedly, without clinging to preconceived notions or desires for a specific gender. Instead of pressuring your spouse to keep having children in pursuit of a particular outcome, you accept the blessings you've received with gratitude, recognising that each child, regardless of gender, is a precious gift deserving of love and appreciation.

Similarly, consider another scenario where you initially planned to have two children, only to discover that your spouse faces fertility challenges preventing them from conceiving. In such circumstances, flexibility calls for understanding and compassion rather than retreat or despair. Rather than allowing setbacks to dictate your path, being flexible means adjusting your expectations and exploring alternative paths to parenthood, such as adoption or other forms of family building.

In essence, flexibility is not about abandoning our goals or desires but rather about recognising that life is unpredictable, and our ability to adapt and embrace change is key to finding fulfilment and happiness. By cultivating a spirit of flexibility, we can navigate life's uncertainties with wisdom and resilience, embracing the unexpected twists and turns as opportunities for growth and transformation.

Chapter Two

Navigating through family and its dynamic types

In the intricate dynamic of life, family plays a central role, shaping our experiences, values, and relationships. Understanding the dynamics of different family structures—be it the nuclear family, extended family, in-laws, or siblings—is essential for fostering harmony and fulfilment. Here's a closer look at each family type and the wisdom to apply when navigating their complexities:

The Nuclear Family

The nuclear family typically consists of parents and their children living together under one roof. This intimate unit forms the foundation of our upbringing, providing love, support, and guidance. To nurture a fulfilling relationship within the nuclear family, communication and empathy are paramount. Listening to each other's needs, respecting boundaries, and fostering a sense of belonging fosters a strong bond and promotes emotional well-being.

Wisdom Tip: Prioritise quality time together, create meaningful traditions, and openly express appreciation and affection to strengthen family ties.

The Extended Family

Extended families encompass a broader network of relatives beyond the nuclear unit, including grandparents, aunts, uncles, and cousins. This expansive circle offers a rich connections, cultural traditions, and shared history. Embracing the diversity within the extended family fosters a sense of belonging and collective support. However be mindful of its challenges that it brings.

Wisdom Tip: Cultivate a spirit of inclusivity, celebrate shared milestones, and maintain open lines of communication to bridge generational gaps and forge lasting bonds.

The In-Laws

In-laws are individuals who become part of our family through marriage. Navigating relationships with in-laws requires tact, patience, and mutual respect. Recognising and honouring the unique dynamics of each family unit while embracing differences can foster harmony and mutual understanding.

Navigating the dynamics of relationships with in-laws can be a journey filled with both blessings and challenges. On one hand, gaining a new family through marriage can bring added love, support, and companionship into your life. On the other hand, differences in values, expectations, and personalities can sometimes lead to friction and conflict. Here, wisdom plays a crucial role in fostering healthy and harmonious relationships with your in-laws.

Firstly, it's essential to approach these relationships with an open heart and mind. Recognise that your in-laws are an integral part of your partner's life and history, and strive to build bridges of understanding and respect. Embrace the blessings of having extended family members who care for

17

you and your partner, and cherish the opportunity to create new memories and traditions together.

At the same time, it's important to establish healthy boundaries and communicate your needs and expectations openly and respectfully. Understand that while your in-laws may have good intentions, they may also have different perspectives and ways of doing things. Be willing to compromise and find common ground, but also assert your boundaries when necessary to maintain your autonomy and individuality within the relationship.

Wisdom also entails practicing empathy and compassion towards your in-laws, recognising that they, too, are navigating the complexities of family dynamics. Seek to understand their perspectives and motivations, and approach conflicts with a spirit of patience and understanding. Remember that every family has its quirks and challenges, and it's okay to disagree as long as it's done with respect and empathy.

Furthermore, prioritise open and honest communication in your interactions with your in-laws. Be willing to address issues and concerns directly and constructively, rather than letting resentment or misunderstandings fester over time. Approach difficult conversations with a spirit of humility and a genuine desire to find solutions that benefit everyone involved.

Let's be honest, there are people who may be difficult to love, and they live their lives in ways that might conflict with yours. The question is, what do you do? Ultimately, you need to fix your eyes on your goal. If that goal is unity, progress, and success, it cannot be achieved with strife or conflict. Strife will hinder that goal. This is where you apply the wisdom described in this book.

Wisdom Tip: Practice active listening, set clear boundaries, and approach conflicts with empathy and diplomacy to cultivate positive relationships with in-laws.

Siblings

Siblings are often our first companions on life's journey, offering both blessings and challenges along the way. While they can provide unwavering support, love, and companionship, they can also test our patience, trigger old rivalries, and sometimes even cause conflict. Here's a look at the blessings and challenges of sibling relationships, along with the wisdom required to navigate them with grace and understanding.

1. *Lifelong Companionship:* Siblings share a unique bond forged by shared experiences, memories, and familial ties. They can offer companionship, empathy, and understanding during life's ups and downs.

2. *Emotional Support:* Siblings often serve as a source of emotional support and comfort during times of need, providing a listening ear and a shoulder to lean on.

3. *Shared Memories:* Growing up together creates a treasure trove of shared memories, from childhood adventures to family traditions, that can strengthen the bond between siblings.

4. *Built-In Support System:* Siblings can provide practical help and assistance in times of need, whether it's lending a hand with household chores, offering financial support, or providing childcare.

Challenges with Siblings

1. *Sibling Rivalry:* Competition, jealousy, and rivalry are common challenges in sibling relationships, especially during childhood and adolescence. Sibling rivalry can lead to conflicts, resentment, and strained relationships if not addressed effectively.

2. *Differences in Personality:* Siblings may have different personalities, interests, and values, leading to misunderstandings and clashes. These differences can create tension and friction within the relationship.

3. *Family Dynamics:* Sibling relationships can be influenced by family dynamics, including parental favouritism, birth order, and family roles. These dynamics can impact the dynamics between siblings and contribute to conflicts and tensions.

4. *Communication Barriers:* Poor communication or unresolved conflicts can strain sibling relationships, leading to misunderstandings, resentment, and distance.

Wisdom Tips:

1. *Cultivate Empathy and Understanding:* Practice empathy and understanding towards your siblings, recognising that they may have their own struggles, insecurities, and perspectives. Seek to understand their point of view and communicate openly and honestly.

2. *Set Boundaries:* Establish healthy boundaries within your sibling relationships, respecting each other's autonomy, privacy, and individuality. Communicate your needs and expectations clearly and assertively, while also respecting the boundaries of others.

3. *Practice Forgiveness:* Let go of past grievances and conflicts, practicing forgiveness and compassion towards your siblings. Holding onto grudges only perpetuates negativity and damages the relationship. Instead, focus on moving forward with a spirit of reconciliation and healing.

4. *Foster Open Communication:* Foster open and honest communication with your siblings, addressing conflicts and concerns directly and constructively. Avoid passive-aggressive behaviours or sweeping issues under the rug, as this can lead to resentment and misunderstanding.

By approaching sibling relationships with wisdom, empathy, and open communication, you can navigate the challenges and embrace the blessings of having siblings in your life.

The place of healthy boundaries

In addition to the wisdom nugget written above, it is very important that you maintain healthy boundaries within family members and not take people for granted. Respecting boundaries between siblings, extended families, and in-laws is paramount to fostering harmonious relationships and avoiding conflict.

Within sibling relationships, it's crucial to recognise and honour each other's autonomy and personal space. While siblings may share a deep bond, it's important to respect individual differences, preferences, and boundaries. Avoiding unnecessary intrusions, respecting privacy, and refraining from overstepping boundaries fosters mutual respect and trust.

Similarly, within extended families, maintaining healthy boundaries is essential for preserving familial harmony. While the extended family offers a wealth of support and connection, respecting each other's autonomy and choices is key. Recognising the importance of individual family units, refraining from unsolicited advice or interference, and communicating openly and respectfully fosters positive relationships and minimizes tension.

When it comes to interactions with in-laws, navigating boundaries requires sensitivity, tact, and mutual respect. Recognising and respecting the unique dynamics of each family unit while maintaining clear boundaries is crucial. Avoiding judgment, refraining from imposing one's own values or beliefs, and communicating openly and respectfully fosters positive relationships and minimizes conflict.

Overall, maintaining healthy boundaries within family relationships requires mindfulness, empathy, and open communication. By respecting each other's autonomy, preferences, and personal space, we can cultivate harmonious relationships built on mutual respect, trust, and understanding.

The marriage wisdom

While I may not hold the title of a marriage counsellor, my near 14-year journey alongside my wife, Lovelyn Eze, and our two children has granted me invaluable experience in the realm of matrimony. Our marriage hasn't been devoid of challenges, yet through mutual understanding, perseverance, and the application of wisdom, we've navigated through disagreements and hurdles, emerging with a deeper understanding and a greater appreciation for each other.

Marriage, as I've come to understand it, is a beautiful union between two unique individuals who come together to share their lives and purpose. However, the path to marital bliss is not without its trials. Without the application of adequate wisdom, couples may find themselves grappling with issues that, if left unaddressed, can strain the relationship and even lead to its dissolution.

In delving into the subject of marriage, it's essential to acknowledge both its beauty and its challenges. While couples enter into marriage with the intention of experiencing joy and happiness together, it's inevitable that they will encounter moments of disagreement and difficulty along the way. What sets successful marriages apart is not the absence of challenges, but rather the willingness of both partners to work through them with patience, understanding, and a commitment to growth.

Central to the success of any marriage are the foundational principles and laws that govern healthy relationships. These principles find expression in everyday actions such as courtesy, acts of service, expressions of love, thoughtfulness, forgiveness, and mutual respect. By adhering to these principles and incorporating them into your daily lives, couples can foster a deep sense of connection and intimacy that sustains them through both the joys and trials of marriage.

Courtesy serves as a cornerstone of marital harmony, reminding couples to treat each other with kindness, consideration, and respect, even in the midst of disagreement. Acts of service demonstrate a willingness to prioritise the needs and well-being of one's partner, fostering a spirit of selflessness and reciprocity within the relationship.

Love, in its truest form, is not merely a feeling but a deliberate choice to prioritise the happiness and fulfilment of one's spouse. Thoughtfulness involves being attuned to your partner's needs and desires, taking proactive steps to show affection and appreciation in meaningful ways.

Forgiveness is perhaps one of the most powerful tools in the marital toolbox, allowing couples to let go of past hurts and grievances, and move forward with a renewed sense of trust and understanding. Learning to wipe the slate clean and approach each day with a fresh perspective can foster a spirit of renewal and growth within the marriage.

Respect is the foundation upon which all healthy relationships are built, requiring couples to honour each other's perspectives, boundaries, and individuality. Esteeming each other highly and valuing each other's contributions fosters a sense of mutual admiration and appreciation that strengthens the marital bond.

As I reflect on my own journey in marriage, I am reminded of the profound wisdom and insight that can be gained through shared experiences and the commitment to weather life's storms together. While challenges may arise, it is the application of wisdom and the unwavering dedication to love, honour, and cherish one another that ultimately defines the success of a marriage.

It is a profound honour to share my thoughts on marriage, recognising that my Journey with my wife is just one part of the many different experiences others have had. My prayer is for couples everywhere to find peace and inspiration in the knowledge that with wisdom, commitment, and love, the joys of marriage far outweigh its challenges, and the bond forged between two hearts can withstand the test of time.

Chapter Three

You are now here in the world
— what next?

Navigating life on planet Earth often feels like running a high hurdle race, with every element of existence seemingly conspiring against us. In reality, we are engaged in a relentless race, contending with our own giants along the way, a test of survival for some and a testament of faith for others. Make no mistake, from the moment we arrive on this planet, we must be prepared to wage war until the day we bid our final farewell.

This isn't a fairy tale or an attempt to instil fear; it's a stark truth. Challenges will inevitably arise as we pursue our dreams and desires.

Consider the scenario where you're vying for a particular goal or aspiration, only to find yourself in competition with others who seek the same outcome. Whether it's pursuing a romantic interest or striving for professional success, there will always be contenders vying for the same prize. In such moments, you're called upon to summon your best qualities—be it your charisma, intellect, or resources *(give treasures in Nigerian terms towards the romantic interest)* —to stand out and achieve your objectives.

At other times, the battle may take the form of illness, requiring a combination of faith, medicine, and the power of positive affirmations and prayers to overcome. Or it may manifest as struggles within relationships or careers, each presenting its own unique battlefield. Yet, regardless of the battlefield, the objective remains the same: victory.

While these battles may not always be physical in nature, their impact can be deeply felt on a personal and emotional level. It's about mustering the courage and determination to confront adversity head-on, armed with the tools and resources at your disposal. Whether it's leveraging your strengths, seeking support from loved ones, or tapping into spiritual guidance, the key is to approach each challenge with a mindset geared towards triumph and growth.

Wisdom Tips

Below are the wisdom tips you may want to engage or put to remembrance when the occasion calls for it.

1. Embrace Challenges: Understand that challenges are a natural part of life's journey. Instead of fearing them, embrace them as opportunities for growth and development.

2. Cultivate Resilience: Develop resilience to bounce back from setbacks and adversities. Remember that setbacks are not permanent, and with perseverance, you can overcome any obstacle.

3. Focus on Your Goals: Stay focused on your goals and aspirations, regardless of the competition or obstacles you may face along the way. Keep your eyes on the prize and channel your energy towards achieving your objectives.

4. Harness Your Strengths: Identify your strengths and leverage them to your advantage. Whether it's your intelligence, creativity, or determination, use your unique qualities to navigate through life's challenges effectively.

5. Seek Support: Don't hesitate to seek support from loved ones or mentors when facing challenges. Surround yourself with a supportive network of individuals who uplift and encourage you during difficult times.

6. Maintain a Positive Mindset: Cultivate a positive mindset that enables you to see challenges as opportunities for growth. Focus on the solutions rather than dwelling on the problems, and approach each situation with optimism and determination.

7. Practice Self-Care: Prioritise self-care and well-being to maintain your physical, mental, and emotional health. Take time to rest, recharge, and engage in activities that bring you joy and fulfilment.

8. Stay Grounded: Stay grounded and connected to your values, beliefs, and principles, even in the face of adversity. Remember what truly matters to you and let it guide your decisions and actions.

9. Embrace Growth: Embrace the process of growth and transformation that comes with overcoming challenges.

Every obstacle you overcome strengthens you and prepares you for future endeavours.

10. *Trust the Journey:* Trust in the journey of life and have faith that everything happens for a reason. Believe in your ability to overcome challenges and emerge stronger and wiser on the other side.

Individual uniqueness, its beauty and challenges

Just like how different our DNA make up is so is how different individuals are, there are good things to it and there are challenges to them. I am sure you are aware but I want this book to highlight and buttress this point in this chapter and the wisdom nuggets that may help you navigate through the complexities that come with individual uniqueness.

Embracing individual uniqueness is akin to celebrating the kaleidoscope of colours in a vibrant mosaic. Each person is endowed with a unique blend of traits, talents, and quirks that make them distinctly themselves. Yet, amidst the beauty of diversity, there are inevitable challenges that arise when navigating the complexities of our own uniqueness and that of others.

The journey of embracing individual uniqueness begins with recognising and honouring the inherent value in each person's distinctiveness. It's about embracing the idiosyncrasies that set us apart and appreciating the richness they bring to our lives and interactions. Whether it's our unique talents, perspectives, or life experiences, these aspects of ourselves shape who we are and contribute to the fabric of our existence.

However, alongside the beauty of individual uniqueness, there can also be challenges that arise. Society often imposes norms and expectations that may conflict with our own sense of identity or authenticity. We may face pressure to conform, to fit into predefined boxes, or to suppress aspects of ourselves that deviate from the norm. These challenges can manifest in various forms, such as societal judgments, self-doubt, or feelings of alienation.

In such moments, wisdom lies in navigating the delicate balance between embracing our uniqueness and navigating the challenges it presents. It requires cultivating self-awareness, self-acceptance, and resilience to stay true to ourselves amidst external pressures.

Wisdom Tips - Here are some wisdom tips to consider:

1. Self-Acceptance: Embrace yourself fully, flaws and all. Recognise that your uniqueness is what makes you special, and celebrate your individuality without seeking validation or approval from others.

2. Authenticity: Stay true to yourself and your values, even when it's challenging or unpopular. Authenticity breeds connection and fosters a sense of belonging, both to yourself and to those who appreciate you for who you truly are.

3. Resilience: Build resilience to overcome obstacles and setbacks that may arise due to your uniqueness. Remember that challenges are opportunities for growth and transformation, and each hurdle you overcome strengthens you for the journey ahead.

4. Compassion: Extend compassion to yourself and others as you navigate the complexities of individual uniqueness. Recognise that everyone is on their own journey, facing their own struggles and insecurities, and approach interactions with empathy and understanding.

5. Seek Support: Surround yourself with a supportive network of friends, family, or mentors who celebrate your uniqueness and uplift you during challenging times. Seek guidance and encouragement from those who appreciate and value you for who you are.

6. Embrace Differences: Embrace the diversity of perspectives and experiences that exist within the human experience. Celebrate the uniqueness of others and cultivate an open-minded and inclusive attitude towards those who may be different from you.

Ultimately, embracing individual uniqueness is a journey of self-discovery, growth, and self-expression. It's about honouring the beauty of diversity, navigating the challenges with grace and wisdom, and embracing the full spectrum of what it means to be uniquely, authentically yourself.

Chapter Four

Wisdom in "Failing fast" and embracing a turnaround positive change

Life on Earth is a profound journey, filled with an abundance of lessons waiting to be learned from the trials and tribulations of both the living and the departed. Failed projects, marriages, careers, and families; accidents, sickness, and struggles—all of these experiences serve as poignant reminders of the fragility and complexity of human existence. Yet, amidst the chaos and turmoil, there lies a treasure trove of wisdom waiting to be unearthed.

One of the greatest challenges we face is our reluctance to heed the lessons that life so graciously offers us. Instead of embracing the opportunity to grow and evolve, we often find ourselves trapped in a cycle of repetition, blindly following in the footsteps of those who came before us. We fail to recognise the signs and signals that point towards a different path. We are too preoccupied with our own desires and ambitions to pause and reflect on the wisdom that surrounds us.

But what if we could learn to fail fast? What if we could cultivate the courage and humility to acknowledge when we're headed down a destructive path and course-correct before it's too late? Failing fast isn't about giving up or admitting defeat; it's about recognising when a particular direction no longer serves us and having the wisdom to pivot towards a more fulfilling and life-affirming path.

For instance, harbouring resentment towards those who have wronged us may feel justified in the moment, but over time, it becomes a poison that eats away at our soul, robbing us of our joy and vitality. By learning to fail fast in resentment, we open ourselves up to the possibility of forgiveness, healing, and freedom. We release ourselves from the burden of carrying grudges and embrace the transformative power of compassion and understanding.

Similarly, in the face of failure or adversity, failing fast allows us to acknowledge our mistakes, learn from them, and move forward with newfound resilience and determination. It's not about avoiding failure altogether, but rather, about embracing it as an essential part of the human experience and using it as a catalyst for growth and self-discovery.

In essence, failing fast is an act of courage and wisdom—an acknowledgment of our fallibility as human beings and a commitment to continuously evolve and improve. It's a reminder that life's greatest lessons often come from our darkest moments, and that by embracing change and learning from our experiences, we can unlock the true potential of our existence.

Virtue- A wise word that is seldom used

When we contemplate the concept of virtue, we are delving into the essence of what it means to be truly human. Virtue is not merely a superficial trait; rather, it is the bedrock upon which a meaningful and positive life is built. It encompasses a myriad of qualities and attributes that guide our actions, shape our character, and define our interactions with the world around us.

At its core, virtue embodies the noblest aspects of humanity—**love**, **patience**, **faithfulness**, **perseverance**, **peace**, **joy**, **kindness**, **self-control**, **gentleness**, and **empathy**. These virtues serve as guiding principles, illuminating the path towards a life of fulfilment and purpose. They are not just abstract ideals, but tangible expressions of our innermost values and beliefs.

Consider **love** as a virtue—a force that transcends boundaries and unites us in compassion and understanding. **Patience**, too, is a virtue that teaches us the value of restraint and tolerance in the face of adversity. Faithfulness instils in us a sense of commitment and loyalty, while perseverance empowers us to overcome obstacles and pursue our dreams with unwavering determination.

Peace and joy, as virtues, remind us of the importance of inner tranquillity and contentment, even amidst life's storms. Kindness, self-control, gentleness, and empathy foster harmonious relationships and promote empathy and understanding towards others.

The absence of virtue, conversely, can lead to a myriad of negative consequences. A lack of love breeds division and conflict, while impatience fuels frustration and resentment. Unfaithfulness erodes trust and undermines the fabric of relationships, and a lack of perseverance stifles personal growth and progress.

In contemplating the impact of virtue on society, it becomes clear that individuals who embody virtuous qualities are the bedrock of a healthy and thriving community. A courteous character fosters cooperation, respect, and mutual support, laying the foundation for a harmonious and inclusive society.

However, in our fast-paced and often turbulent world, the importance of cultivating virtues is sometimes overlooked or overshadowed by other pursuits. Yet, it is precisely in times of uncertainty and stress that the virtues of patience, resilience, and empathy become most essential.

Today, I urge you to reflect on the virtues that resonate most deeply with your soul and strive to embody them in your daily life. For in embracing virtue, we not only enrich our own lives but also contribute to the collective well-being of humanity.

Wisdom in delayed gratification

Delayed gratification is the ability to resist immediate rewards for greater future benefits. It means focusing on long-term goals and benefits instead of short-term pleasures. Whilst challenging, it offers profound benefits.

Delayed gratification requires self-control and patience. It's about making conscious decisions to forego immediate satisfaction in favour of future gains. This concept is widely recognised in various fields, including psychology, finance, and personal development, as a critical component of success and well-being.

Benefits of Delayed Gratification

1. *Financial Stability:* One of the most evident benefits of delayed gratification is financial stability. By resisting impulsive purchases and unnecessary expenditures, individuals can save and invest money, leading to greater financial security and the ability to achieve larger financial goals, such as buying a home or retiring comfortably.

2. *Personal Growth:* Practicing delayed gratification fosters discipline and self-control. These qualities are essential for personal growth and the pursuit of long-term aspirations. Individuals who master this skill are often more focused, determined, and capable of overcoming obstacles.

3. *Better Health:* Delayed gratification is linked to healthier lifestyle choices. For example, choosing to eat nutritious food rather than indulging in junk food, or committing to regular exercise despite the immediate allure of a sedentary lifestyle, can lead to improved physical and mental health.

4. Stronger Relationships: In relationships, the ability to delay gratification can lead to more meaningful and lasting connections. Prioritising the long-term health of a relationship over short-term desires helps build trust and mutual respect.

My Experience

Once upon a time, I had the opportunity to live in a self-contained studio apartment as a single young man in the UK. The allure of having my own space was strong, but the cost was twice that of living in a shared house. My goal was to save money for other projects, and moving into the studio apartment would have significantly hindered my financial plans.

Although it was tempting to enjoy the immediate comfort and privacy of my own apartment, I chose to live in a shared house. This decision allowed me to save a substantial amount of money, which I later invested in projects that had a more significant impact on my life and career.

Delayed Gratification in Entrepreneurship

For entrepreneurs, delayed gratification is crucial. Starting a business requires substantial capital, and using this capital for personal pleasures rather than investing it back into the business can jeopardise the venture. Entrepreneurs who practice delayed gratification are more likely to see their businesses succeed, as they are willing to make short-term sacrifices for long-term gains. I grew up surrounded by businessmen, including my dad and my uncles, and the principle of delayed gratification always applied. There is a saying in Igbo, one of the major languages of Nigeria, which goes, "Ji na adi n'oba, aguru na agukwa." Translated into English, it means, "You have yams in the barn and are still hungry." This proverb illustrates that the owner of the yams understands that they are meant for planting, not for immediate consumption. It reflects a deeper wisdom about the importance of foresight and delayed gratification, emphasising the value of preserving resources for future sustainability rather than using them up for short-term gain.

Delayed gratification in Relationships

In relationships, the inability to delay gratification can lead to dissatisfaction and instability. For example, a couple might choose to forgo immediate luxuries to save for a down payment on a house. This decision requires patience and mutual support, ultimately leading to a more stable and fulfilling relationship.

To wrap this section, I would like to bring to your utmost awareness that delayed gratification is an integral part of success in various aspects of life. It requires discipline, patience, and a clear vision of long-term goals. By resisting the temptation of immediate rewards, individuals can achieve greater financial stability, personal growth, better health, stronger relationships, and entrepreneurial success. The ability to delay gratification is a powerful tool that, when mastered, can significantly enhance one's quality of life and lead to lasting fulfilment.

Having talked about delayed gratification and its benefits, I would like to also mention that not every scenario should be approached with delayed gratification, especially when an *opportunity is unique* and *unlikely to recur*. I have put those two phrases in italics because they are key determinants to when a situation is not supposed to be delayed. Here is an example illustrating such scenario:

Scenario: In delayed gratification

Obioma (A Nigerian name. Pronounced as O be Or Ma) works in a mid-level management position at a reputable company. She is offered a rare opportunity to lead a high-profile project that could significantly advance her career, but it requires her to relocate to a different country for a year. Obioma hesitates because she had planned to pursue an executive MBA program the following year, believing it would boost her long-term career prospects.

Analysis:

In this scenario, if Obioma chooses to delay taking the project for the sake of her education, she might miss out on this unique opportunity that offers immediate career advancement and practical experience that could surpass the benefits of an MBA. The project may also provide her with networking opportunities and professional growth that are irreplaceable. Here, not taking the opportunity could mean sacrificing a one-time chance that might not present itself again.

Chapter Five

The Mind: Your Master Key to a Fulfilling Life

In life, our mind acts like a conductor, guiding how we experience everything around us. It is the master key that opens the door to a multitude of outcomes – from joy and satisfaction to depression and failure. Understanding the profound influence of the mind and nurturing its health and vitality is paramount to unlocking the full potential of our lives.

The mind is not merely a passive observer of our experiences; it is an active participant, shaping our thoughts, emotions, and actions. Like a sponge, it absorbs and retains the impressions of our daily encounters, moulding our perceptions and influencing our behaviours. Therefore, it is imperative to treat the mind with the care and attention it deserves, just as we would tend to a prized possession.

Nourishing the mind begins with conscious awareness and deliberate effort. Just as we feed our bodies with nutritious food to maintain physical health, we must nourish our minds with positive thoughts, uplifting experiences, and enriching knowledge. Regular visits to the "mind health clinics" – be it through meditation, mindfulness practices, or therapy – can help cleanse and rejuvenate the mind, ensuring its optimal functioning.

Moreover, the mind is a fertile ground for seeds of truth and wisdom to take root and flourish. By consciously educating ourselves and exposing our minds to the school of positive affirmation, we empower ourselves to challenge limiting beliefs and cultivate a mindset of abundance and growth. Through affirmations and self-talk, we can steer the course of our thoughts in a direction that serves our highest good, fostering resilience and inner strength.

Indeed, the mind is a powerful influencer, shaping the trajectory of our lives and championing what becomes of us. It is not merely a passive recipient of external stimuli but an active agent in the creation of our reality. Therefore, it is essential to pay great attention to the dialogue we engage in with our minds, reprimanding and correcting it when it veers off course.

In navigating the complexities of life, our minds serve as both compass and rudder, guiding us through the ebb and flow of our experiences. By cultivating a mindful awareness of our thoughts and emotions, we can harness the transformative power of the mind to navigate life's challenges with grace and resilience.

In addition to the profound influence of the mind on our lives, it's essential to recognise that our minds can often lead us astray if left unchecked. Many individuals have fallen victim to the deceptive whispers of their own minds, succumbing to false beliefs and negative self-talk that have ultimately led them down a path of despair and disillusionment.

To guard against the pitfalls of the mind, it's crucial to enlist the support of mentors who can help navigate the turbulent waters of our thoughts. These mentors serve as beacons of wisdom, offering guidance and clarity amidst the chaos of our minds. Through their words of encouragement and insight, they can help dispel the clouds of confusion and lead us towards a path of truth and enlightenment.

Furthermore, we must learn to engage in positive self-talk and affirmations, consciously directing our inner dialogue towards thoughts of empowerment and self-belief. By speaking to ourselves with kindness and compassion, we can counteract the negative chatter of the mind and cultivate a mindset of resilience and inner strength.

Indeed, the battle for control of our minds is an ongoing struggle, one that requires constant vigilance and mindfulness. It's essential to recognise that we are at war with our minds, and it's only through diligent effort and intentional practice that we can emerge victorious.

Thus, while the mind serves as the master key to a fulfilling life, it also poses significant challenges that must be addressed. By surrounding ourselves with mentors who can offer guidance and support, and by engaging in positive self-talk and affirmations, we can safeguard our minds against the dangers of negative thinking and cultivate a mindset of positivity and empowerment. Let us embark on this journey of self-discovery and transformation, armed with the knowledge that we have the power to shape our reality and create the life we truly desire.

The mindset in knowing your challenge is not unique to you

Having a mindset that your challenge or problem is not unique to you will help you realise that someone out there has faced something similar and overcome it. This realisation can be incredibly encouraging and empowering, as it reminds you that you are not alone in your struggles and that solutions and paths to success have already been forged by others.

In the vast mosaic of human experience, there exists a timeless truth encapsulated in the phrase, "there is nothing new under the sun." It's a sentiment that echoes through the corridors of time, reminding us that while our individual experiences may feel unique, they are often variations of universal themes that have played out countless times before.

Consider the myriad of emotions we encounter in our daily lives – joy, sorrow, love, fear. While the circumstances that evoke these emotions may differ from person to person, the essence of the human experience remains unchanged. Pain, for example, may manifest differently from one individual to another, but its presence is a shared reality of the human condition.

In recognising the universality of human experience, we gain a broader perspective on the challenges we face. Rather than viewing our struggles as isolated incidents, we understand them as part of the larger fabric of life – a fabric woven with threads of triumph and adversity, joy and sorrow.

Indeed, life's challenges can be categorised into two broad categories: *those that are outside of our control* and *those that are within our control* but requires wisdom to navigate. Whether it's facing a sudden loss, navigating a difficult relationship, or grappling with unforeseen circumstances, we are often confronted with situations that test our resilience and fortitude.

Yet, even in the face of adversity, there is solace to be found in the knowledge that nothing lasts forever. Just as the seasons change and the tides ebb and flow, so too do life's trials and tribulations. Each challenge is time-tagged and seasonal, with an expiration date that reminds us of the transient nature of our experiences.

In navigating life's challenges, we can draw inspiration from the wisdom of those who have gone before us. Across cultures and generations, the virtues of patience, self-control, persistence, and hope have been celebrated as guiding lights in times of darkness. Whether it's weathering the storm with grace and resilience or holding onto hope for a better tomorrow, this wisdom serves as a beacon of light, illuminating the path forward.

So, the next time you find yourself facing adversity, remember the timeless truth encapsulated in the phrase, "there is nothing new under the sun." Embrace the challenges before you with courage and resilience, knowing that you walk in the footsteps of countless others who have journeyed this path before. And as you navigate life's twists and turns, may you find solace in the knowledge that every trial is but a season, and every challenge is an opportunity for growth and transformation.

Walk the path of giants and become one

Wisdom dictates that we look to the giants who have walked before us, those remarkable individuals whose footsteps have left indelible marks on the sands of time. Men and women of great exploits and noble character have blazed countless trails, carving paths through the wilderness of life that we now have the privilege to follow.

In our pursuit of success and fulfilment, there is no need to reinvent the wheel when we can glean valuable insights and wisdom from these giants. While some may boast of being "self-made," the truth is that every individual, from the moment of conception to the present day, has been shaped and influenced by the guidance and support of others. Whether it be the nurturing care of parents, the wisdom imparted by teachers, or the mentorship of respected elders, our journey is marked by the contributions of those who have come before us.

Take a moment to look around you, and you will undoubtedly find individuals whose lives inspire and captivate your imagination. Perhaps it is a successful entrepreneur who has built a thriving business from the ground up, or a renowned artist whose creations stir the soul. Whatever the case may be, these individuals offer valuable lessons and examples that we can emulate on our own journey to success.

The key to learning from these giants lies in observing their actions, dissecting their strategies, and discerning the principles that underpin their success. Success, after all, leaves behind a trail of breadcrumbs for those who are willing to follow. By studying the examples, clues, and footprints left by these trailblazers, we can gain invaluable insights into what it takes to achieve greatness.

But it's not enough to simply mimic the actions of those who have gone before us. True wisdom lies in taking what we have learned from these giants and building upon it, forging our own path to success. It's about recognising that while we may stand on the shoulders of giants, we also have the capacity to reach even greater heights.

In conclusion, the wisdom in learning from giants is undeniable. By studying the lives and achievements of those who have come before us, we can gain valuable insights and guidance that will propel us forward on our own journey to success. Let us not shy away from the wisdom that surrounds us, but instead, let us embrace it wholeheartedly as we strive to reach our fullest potential.

The wisdom in Honour

Honour can be defined as a profound sense of ethical conduct, respect, and esteem for others. It involves recognising the inherent worth and dignity of individuals and acting in ways that reflect this recognition. Honour is not merely an internal feeling but is demonstrated through actions that show respect and esteem for others.

Honouring others is a wise practice for several reasons:

1. Strengthening Relationships: Honour fosters mutual respect and trust, which are foundational for healthy and lasting relationships. By honouring others, you create a positive and supportive environment where relationships can thrive.

2. Creating a Positive Reputation: Individuals who consistently show honour are viewed as trustworthy and respectable. This reputation can open doors to opportunities and networks that might otherwise be inaccessible.

3. Promoting Social Harmony: Honour contributes to a culture of respect and civility. When people honour each other, conflicts are less likely to escalate, and communities can function more smoothly.

4. Encouraging Reciprocity: Honour often begets honour. When you honour others, you set a standard of behaviour that encourages them to reciprocate. This reciprocal respect can lead to mutually beneficial interactions and collaborations.

The Honour effect

Who you honour can significantly influence the blessings and favour you receive. Conversely, who you dishonour can determine the opportunities and goodwill you might miss out on. Here's why:

1. *Attracting Favour:* When you honour others, especially those who have earned respect through their actions and character, you are likely to attract their favour and goodwill. This can manifest in various forms, such as mentorship, support, and opportunities that might not have been available otherwise.

2. *Avoiding Missed Opportunities:* Dishonouring others can close doors and lead to missed blessings. People are less likely to extend help, opportunities, or goodwill to those who have shown them disrespect.

Let's have a look at a scenario relating to honour in attracting favour and avoiding missed opportunities so as to drive the "nail" home

Scenario : Honour effect

John is a graduate student working on a complex research project. He consistently shows respect and admiration for a well-established professor who has made significant contributions to his field of study. John attends the professor's lectures, actively participates in discussions, and often seeks their advice on his research. He expresses genuine gratitude for their guidance and acknowledges their influence on his academic progress during seminars and conferences.

Over time, the professor notices John's respect and dedication. When an opportunity for a mentorship program arises, the professor immediately thinks of John. They advocate for him, placing him on the selection panel and writing a strong letter of recommendation. As a result, John secures a spot in the prestigious mentoring program, significantly advancing his academic and professional development..

Honour as a Mark of Respect

Honour is not about seeking self-glorification but about recognising and valuing others. It is given not out of self-interest but because the person being honoured deserves it. For example, giving up your seat on a bus for an elderly person is an act of honour. This act is not about seeking praise but about respecting the dignity and needs of the elderly person.

Let's look at practical examples illustrating what respect means in the context of honour:

1. *Listening and Valuing Input:* In a team meeting, when someone shares an idea or expresses a concern, honouring them involves actively listening, considering their input, and valuing their perspective. This demonstrates respect for their contributions to the discussion, regardless of their position or rank within the team.

2. *Acknowledging Achievements:* When someone achieves a milestone or accomplishes a task, honouring them means acknowledging their efforts and celebrating their success. This can be done publicly, such as in a company-wide email or during a team meeting, to show appreciation for their hard work and dedication.

3. _Showing Gratitude:_ Honouring someone also involves expressing gratitude for their presence, support, or assistance. This could be as simple as saying "thank you" for a small favour or expressing heartfelt appreciation for their ongoing support and friendship. Showing gratitude demonstrates respect for their kindness and generosity.

Neglecting these wisdoms could become your stumbling block or something that impede your progress.

The Irresistible Fragrance of Honour

Honour has an irresistible fragrance that provokes others to bless you. This metaphorical fragrance stems from the genuine respect and kindness inherent in honourable actions. In a time when self-glorification often overshadows selflessness, honour stands out as a refreshing and noble practice.

By practising honour, you cultivate a character that attracts positive attention and goodwill. People are naturally drawn to those who demonstrate respect and integrity, leading to a cycle of blessings and favour that can significantly enrich your life and the lives of those around you.

Scenario: Attracting Goodwill

Amina, a diligent employee at a prominent firm, exemplifies honour in her interactions with her boss and colleagues. She consistently demonstrates respect and appreciation for their efforts and expertise. Whenever her boss's workload becomes overwhelming, Amina gladly volunteers to take on additional responsibilities, ensuring that tasks are completed efficiently and deadlines are met. Moreover, Amina's considerate nature extends beyond the workplace; she often gives up her seat on public transportation to ensure the comfort of others, especially elderly or pregnant individuals.

Amina's boss recognises and appreciates her exemplary behaviour, praising her respect and honour to colleagues both within and outside the company. Word spreads about Amina's commendable attitude, reaching even those beyond her immediate professional circle.

During a crucial job interview, Amina's reputation precedes her. The interviewer, having heard about Amina's respectful demeanour from mutual connections, is impressed by her character even before meeting her in person. Amina's honourable conduct becomes an added goodwill, speaking volumes about her professionalism and integrity. As a result, Amina not only excels in the interview but also secures the job opportunity, with her good attitude serving as a testament to her capabilities and character

Chapter Six

Close the doors against strife

In this chapter, we delve into the concept of strife, particularly within the intricate dynamics of families and organisations. Strife, in its essence, is a state of conflict, discord, or disagreement that disrupts the harmony and peace within a group or entity. It can arise from various sources, including differences in opinions, values, or goals, and if left unchecked, it has the potential to sow seeds of division and hinder progress.

Within the context of family or organisational dynamics, strife can be particularly insidious. It has the power to fracture relationships, undermine trust, and create an atmosphere of tension and animosity. As the saying goes, "a house divided against itself cannot stand," highlighting the destructive nature of strife and its ability to erode the very foundation upon which unity and progress are built.

Indeed, strife has the potential to unravel all the hard work and dedication invested in nurturing healthy relationships and fostering a collaborative environment. It can derail even the most well-intentioned endeavours, leaving behind a trail of bitterness and resentment in its wake.

So, how can we safeguard against the corrosive influence of strife and preserve the peace and harmony within our families and organisations? The answer lies in embracing a wisdom-centric approach to conflict resolution and relationship management.

First and foremost, it's essential to recognise the warning signs of strife and address them proactively. Whether it's a simmering disagreement between family members or tension brewing within a team, acknowledging the presence of strife is the first step towards resolution.

Next, we must identify the root causes of strife and work towards addressing them with compassion and understanding. Often, strife arises from miscommunication, unmet expectations, or unresolved conflicts, and by fostering open and honest dialogue, we can begin to bridge the divide and heal rifts.

Furthermore, it's crucial to cultivate emotional intelligence and self-awareness, particularly in moments of heightened tension or conflict. Rather than reacting impulsively or allowing emotions to escalate, we can choose to respond with patience, empathy, and grace. Sometimes, this may involve taking a step back, closing our mouths, or removing ourselves from the environment until emotions have cooled.

Ultimately, the path to avoiding strife lies in cultivating a culture of respect, empathy, and collaboration within our families and organisations. By prioritising open communication, active listening, and mutual understanding, we can create an environment where conflicts are addressed constructively, and relationships are strengthened rather than strained.

Finally, let us heed the wisdom that teaches us to close every door to strife, recognising its destructive potential and choosing instead to embrace peace, harmony, and unity. By doing so, we not only safeguard our relationships and organisations but also pave the way for a brighter, more prosperous future for all.

Strife in family

Strife, like a stealthy thief in the night, has a way of creeping into our families when we least expected it. What may start as minor disagreements or misunderstandings can quickly escalate into heated arguments, resentment, and discord. Yet, amidst the chaos, it's essential to remember the sacred bond that unites us with our loved ones – the promise of alliance, mutual support, and shared progress.

In our journey through marriage and family life, my wife and I have faced challenges as stated earlier. There have been times when disagreements have led into more misunderstandings requiring patience and understanding to resolve. **However, we've come to realise that acknowledging any conflicts, wrongs, or their sources is the first step towards resolving them.**

One of the keys to addressing strife within the family is identifying its root causes. Often, strife arises from unmet expectations, unresolved conflicts, or a lack of effective communication. By delving beneath the surface and exploring the underlying issues, we can begin to unravel the tangled threads of discord and pave the way for reconciliation.

For example, consider a scenario where tension arises between spouses due to differences in parenting styles. Rather than allowing this tension to fester and escalate, it's crucial to engage in open and honest dialogue, seeking to understand each other's perspectives and find common ground. This may involve setting aside time to discuss parenting strategies, clarifying roles and responsibilities, and establishing clear boundaries and expectations.

Similarly, financial disagreements can also become sources of strife within the family. Whether it's disagreements over spending habits, budgeting priorities, or long-term financial goals, it's essential to approach these discussions with patience, empathy, and a willingness to compromise. By working together to create a shared vision for financial stability and prosperity, families can avoid unnecessary conflict and strengthen their financial well-being.

In addition to addressing specific issues, it's crucial to cultivate a culture of respect, kindness, and appreciation within the family. Simple gestures like expressing gratitude, showing empathy, and offering words of encouragement can go a long way in fostering a sense of unity and harmony. Remember, where there is unity, blessings abound, but where there is strife, your blessings develop wings and fly away like birds.

Therefore, let us heed the wisdom that teaches us to guard our homes against the insidious influence of strife. By recognising its presence, addressing its root causes, and cultivating a culture of love and respect, we can create a sanctuary of peace and harmony where our families can thrive and flourish.

Strife in Organisation

Strife within organizations, like a silent saboteur, often infiltrates unnoticed until its effects become evident through diminished productivity, lowered morale, and disrupted team dynamics. What might begin as minor disagreements or differing viewpoints can rapidly escalate into significant conflicts, resulting in a toxic work environment. To navigate and mitigate organizational strife, it is crucial to recognize its presence, understand its root causes, and adopt effective strategies for resolution.

Sources of Strife in Organisation

Strife in an organization typically stems from a variety of sources, including:

1. Communication Breakdowns: Misunderstandings or lack of clear communication can lead to confusion and frustration among team members.

2. Divergent Goals: Conflicts may arise when individual or departmental goals are misaligned with the organization's objectives.

3. Resource Competition: Limited resources can create a competitive environment, fostering resentment and rivalry.

4. Personality Clashes: Differences in personalities and work styles can cause friction and disrupt teamwork.

5. Power Struggles: Disputes over authority and decision-making power can lead to significant strife.

Scenario: In project environment

Consider a scenario where a project team is experiencing tension due to differing opinions on the project's direction. The project manager, Adejumoke,(A Nigerian name pronounced as Ah- day-Jew-Mo- oh- kay) believes in a traditional approach, focusing on tried-and-tested methods. Meanwhile, another team member, Jamie, advocates for a more innovative and risky strategy. The disagreement between Adejumoke and Jamie begins to affect the entire team, causing delays and diminishing team morale.

In this situation, addressing the root causes of the conflict is essential. Here's how the organization can effectively manage the strife:

1. Open Dialogue: Adejumoke and Jamie need to engage in a constructive conversation to understand each other's perspectives. Facilitating a meeting where both parties can express their views and concerns without interruption is crucial

2. _Mediation:_ Involving a neutral third party, such as an HR representative or an external mediator, can help navigate the discussion, ensuring it remains productive and focused on finding a resolution

3. _Aligning Goals:_ It's vital to realign the team's goals with the organization's objectives. By highlighting the common goal of the project's success, Adejumoke and Jamie can find common ground and work towards a shared vision.

4. _Clarifying Roles:_ Clear delineation of roles and responsibilities can prevent future misunderstandings. Adejumoke and Jamie should outline their specific contributions to the project, ensuring there is no overlap or ambiguity.

5. _Continuous Feedback:_ Establishing a culture of continuous feedback can help pre-empt conflicts. Regular check-ins and feedback sessions can address issues before they escalate.

Chapter Seven

Navigating Life's Terrain
— Physical and Spiritual

You must understand that life is a multifaceted journey, encompassing both the physical and the spiritual realms. In this earthly existence, you inhabit a body with a soul, but you are also a spiritual being, connected to a realm beyond the tangible world. While the physical aspect of life is readily apparent through the five senses—smell, touch, hearing, sight, and taste—there exists a deeper, more profound dimension: the spiritual.

Beyond the confines of the physical world lies the realm of the soul and spirit. These ethereal components of your being serve as guides, helping you navigate the complexities of life and directing your path on this earthly journey. However, tapping into the power of your spirit requires a conscious effort and a willingness to delve into the unseen realm.

Central to both the physical and spiritual aspects of existence are the fundamental concepts of laws and principles. Just as there are natural laws governing the physical universe—such as the laws of gravity and motion— there are also spiritual laws and eternal principles that govern the spiritual realm. Understanding and aligning yourself with these laws and principles is essential for a harmonious and prosperous life.

Living in harmony with the laws and principles of both the physical and spiritual worlds is crucial for your well-being and success. When you collaborate with these universal truths, you tap into a source of wisdom and guidance that can propel you forward on your journey. However, disregarding or violating these laws can have dire consequences, leading to disharmony, suffering, and spiritual unrest.

Therefore, it is imperative to cultivate an awareness of the laws and principles that govern both realms and to strive to live in accordance with them. By doing so, you not only enhance your physical and spiritual well-being but also align yourself with the greater purpose and order of the universe.

The place of laws and principles in the outcomes of our lives

Delving deeper into the concept of laws and principles that govern our physical and spiritual worlds opens the door to a profound understanding of how they shape every aspect of human endeavour. These universal truths serve as guiding principles that influence our actions, decisions, and ultimately, our outcomes in life. By recognising and applying these laws and principles, we can harness their transformative power to achieve success and fulfilment in various areas of our lives.

One such area where the application of laws and principles is crucial is in the realm of financial success. There exist fundamental laws and principles that govern the process of wealth creation and accumulation. Understanding these principles, such as the law of abundance and the principle of compounding, allows individuals to navigate the world of finance with clarity and purpose. By aligning their actions with these principles, individuals can attract wealth and abundance into their lives and achieve financial freedom.

Similarly, the quest for longevity and well-being is governed by its own set of laws and principles. From the importance of nutrition and exercise to the role of stress management and emotional well-being, there are universal truths that dictate the path to a long and healthy life. By adhering to these principles, individuals can optimise their physical and mental health, increase their life expectancy, and enjoy a higher quality of life well into old age.

In exploring these laws and principles, it becomes evident that they are not arbitrary or capricious; rather, they are rooted in the fundamental order of the universe. Just as the laws of physics govern the motion of celestial bodies, the laws and principles that govern human endeavour are immutable and unwavering. They operate regardless of one's beliefs or circumstances, acting as guiding beacons that illuminate the path to success and fulfilment.

Moreover, the application of these laws and principles is not limited to specific fields or endeavours; rather, they transcend boundaries and apply universally to all aspects of life. Whether in business, relationships, health, or personal development, the same fundamental truths hold sway, offering a blueprint for success and prosperity.

In the subchapter focusing on longevity and well-being, we will delve deeper into the specific laws and principles that govern health and longevity. From the importance of proper nutrition and regular exercise to the role of stress management and emotional resilience, we will explore how adherence to these principles can enhance overall well-being and increase life expectancy.

The recognition and application of the laws and principles that govern our physical and spiritual worlds are essential for achieving success and fulfilment in life. By aligning our actions with these universal truths, we can unlock our full potential, overcome obstacles, and create the life we desire. Through continued study, reflection, and application, we can harness the transformative power of these laws and principles to lead lives of purpose, abundance, and joy.

The laws and principles that govern longevity

In the journey towards achieving longevity and vibrant health, the application of certain laws and principles plays a pivotal role in shaping our physical and emotional well-being. These laws and principles act as guiding light, directing us towards a life of harmony, health, and vitality. From the intricate workings of our cells and organs to the profound impact of our thoughts and words, each aspect of our being is governed by these fundamental truths.

Proper nutrition and regular exercise are among the cornerstone principles that contribute to longevity and well-being. The food we consume serves as fuel for our bodies, providing essential nutrients that support optimal functioning and cellular repair. By nourishing ourselves with wholesome, nutrient-rich foods, we not only fuel our physical bodies but also lay the foundation for long-term health and vitality.

Similarly, regular exercise is vital for maintaining a strong and resilient body. Physical activity helps to strengthen muscles, improve cardiovascular health, and enhance overall mobility and flexibility. By incorporating regular exercise into our daily routines, we can ward off chronic diseases, boost our immune system, and increase our life expectancy.

Yet, the quest for longevity extends beyond the realm of physical health to encompass the importance of emotional well-being and stress management. Chronic stress has been linked to a host of health problems, including heart disease, diabetes, and depression. Therefore, cultivating emotional resilience and adopting healthy coping mechanisms are essential for promoting overall well-being and longevity.

In addition to these well-known principles, there exists another fundamental law that is often overlooked but holds profound implications for our health and longevity: the law of the tongue. The power of life and death is said to reside in the words we speak (Proverbs 18 :21), highlighting the profound impact of our thoughts and words on our physical and emotional well-being.

Indeed, the words we speak have the power to shape our reality, influencing our thoughts, emotions, and actions. When we speak words of negativity, fear, and doubt, we reinforce patterns of sickness and disease in our bodies. Conversely, when we speak words of positivity, faith, and affirmation, we invite health, vitality, and long life into our lives.

Therefore, it is imperative that we guard our lips and tongues, being mindful of the words we speak and the energy they carry. By choosing to speak words of life, health, and abundance, we can harness the power of our words to create the life we desire. Through conscious awareness and intentional speech, we can align ourselves with the laws and principles that govern longevity and well-being, setting ourselves on a path towards a long, healthy, and fulfilling life.

Chapter Eight

The wisdom in Courage

If you have lived long enough on earth, and by that, I mean you are not newly born, you will realise that you have faced problems and challenges. Some of these, you may have invited through your mistakes or behaviours, while others were thrust upon you by chance. Regardless of their origin, these obstacles are an inherent part of the human experience. I will classify all of these as problems or challenges.

These challenges, whether mundane or monumental, shape our journey and define our resilience. Problems are an inescapable aspect of existence, arising from our interactions with the world and others, from the complexities of nature, and from the depths of our own minds. They are the trials that test our mettle, the obstacles that demand our ingenuity and perseverance. Yet, it is not merely the presence of problems that matters, but our response to them that truly defines us.

Take a moment and reflect on your life, the challenges that you have faced and what the key factor was that enabled you to overcome them. I am sure courage is key. Whether it was overcoming a personal loss, facing a daunting career setback, or navigating through a major life transition, courage likely played a pivotal role in your ability to move forward.

At the heart of this response lies courage. Courage is the force that propels us to face the unknown, to tackle difficulties head-on, and to venture into uncharted territories. It is the inner strength that empowers us to confront the problems we cannot foresee and to overcome those we cannot avoid. Courage is not the absence of fear, but the will to act in spite of it. It is the resolve to pursue solutions, to endure hardships, and to rise above adversities.

Consider the scenario of a young professional named Alex. After years of dedication and hard work, Alex finally lands a dream job. However, a few months into the role, the company faces severe financial difficulties, and layoffs seem imminent. Alex has two choices: succumb to the fear of losing the job or courageously seek solutions. Choosing the latter, Alex proposes innovative cost-saving measures and identifies new business opportunities. Although the fear of failure looms large, Alex's courage to act not only saved the job but also positions Alex as a valuable asset to the company.

In another scenario, imagine Maria, a single mother struggling to make ends meet. Her daily life is fraught with challenges, from juggling multiple jobs to ensuring her children receive a good education. Maria's courage is her lifeline. Instead of being overwhelmed by her circumstances, she decides to further her education, attending classes to secure a better-paying job. Her relentless pursuit of a better life, despite the exhaustion and countless hurdles, not only transforms her own future but also sets a powerful example for her children about the importance of perseverance and courage.

In the face of inevitable problems, courage acts as a catalyst for growth. It drives us to innovate, to learn, and to evolve. When we dare to confront challenges, we expand our horizons and unlock our potential. Problems become opportunities for development, teaching us valuable lessons and equipping us with the skills and wisdom needed for future endeavours. Courage transforms obstacles into stepping stones, guiding us toward a more profound understanding of ourselves and the world around us.

Moreover, courage fosters resilience. In a world where problems are unavoidable, the ability to bounce back from setbacks is crucial. Courageous individuals possess the tenacity to persevere, to adapt, and to keep moving forward despite the odds. They are not deterred by failure, but rather view it as a temporary detour on the path to success. This resilience is the bedrock of personal growth and the foundation of a fulfilling life.

Courage also inspires others. Acts of bravery, whether grand or subtle, have a ripple effect, encouraging those around us to face their own challenges. When we demonstrate courage, we create a culture of strength and determination, fostering a community where problems are tackled collectively and with greater efficacy.

To wrap up this chapter, it is very important that you are made aware that problems are an inescapable part of life, but it is our courage that defines our response to them. Courage empowers us to confront the inevitable, to rise above adversity, and to transform challenges into opportunities. It is the driving force that enables us to navigate the complexities of life with grace and resilience. As we embrace courage, we not only overcome the problems we face but also inspire others to do the same, creating a world where challenges are met with unwavering resolve and unyielding hope.

Chapter Nine

The Baton Should Be Passed On

Life is like a relay race, a journey where we pass the baton from one generation to the next, ensuring a seamless transition and continuity of the race. As we approach the end of our own leg of the race, it's crucial to reflect on our journey, acknowledging both our triumphs and our failures, and preparing diligently for the handover of the baton to the next runner.

Just as in any relay race, adequate preparation is key to ensuring a successful handover. In the context of life, this means taking stock of our accomplishments and shortcomings, identifying areas where we excelled and areas where we fell short. It's about recognising the joys we experienced along the way—the moments of triumph, love, and fulfilment—and also acknowledging the challenges we faced, the obstacles we overcame, and the lessons we learned.

In preparing for the handover, there are several key areas to consider. Firstly, in the realm of family, it's essential to pass on not only material possessions but also values, traditions, and wisdom. Share with the next generation the lessons you've learned about love, resilience, integrity, and compassion. Encourage them to embrace these values and carry them forward into the future.

In the corporate world or any professional setting, the handover involves passing on knowledge, expertise, and leadership. Reflect on your successes and failures in your career, the strategies that worked and those that didn't, and impart these insights to your colleagues or mentees. Encourage them to learn from your experiences, to innovate and adapt, and to always strive for excellence.

As you prepare for the handover, be honest about your shortcomings and mistakes, but also celebrate your achievements and victories. Share with the next generation the joys you experienced—the moments of pride, fulfilment, and connection—and inspire them to seek out their own sources of joy and fulfilment in life.

Above all, encourage the next generation to avoid the pitfalls and mistakes you encountered along the way. Warn them against the dangers of complacency, selfishness, and shortsightedness. Teach them the importance of resilience, perseverance, and adaptability in the face of adversity.

In the relay race of life, the handover is not the end of the journey but rather a continuation—a passing of the torch from one runner to the next. By preparing diligently, sharing our wisdom, and guiding the next generation with love and compassion, we can ensure that the race continues, and that each runner has the tools and the strength to run their leg of the race with grace and purpose.

Passing the baton to your family

Passing on the baton to your children or spouse is a profound symbol of unity of purpose and vision. It's akin to the critical moment in a relay race where each runner must flawlessly pass the baton to the next, ensuring the team's success. In life, if one fails, all fail, just as in a relay race. If a racer falters in passing the baton, the entire team's chances of finishing the race diminish.

To pass on the baton effectively to your family, strategic planning and execution are paramount. Much like in a relay race, meticulous preparation is required to achieve the desired goal. It's essential to start this process early, not waiting until age or circumstance begins to limit your capacity. Begin when you're full of energy and vitality, laying the foundation for a seamless transition of responsibilities and legacies.

By adopting a proactive approach and initiating this process in a timely manner, you can ensure that your family's journey continues with purpose and direction. Whether it's imparting wisdom, sharing experiences, or fostering unity among family members, every action taken in passing on the baton contributes to the collective success and fulfilment of your family's vision. So, seize the opportunity to lead by example and empower future generations to carry on the legacy with grace and resilience.

Consequences of not passing on the baton

Consequences of not passing the baton effectively within the family can have significant impacts on the continuity and success of the family's journey:

1. *Loss of Unity:* Without a clear transition plan or effective passing of the baton, the family may experience a lack of cohesion and unity. This can lead to conflicts, misunderstandings, and divisions among family members, hindering progress towards shared goals.

2. *Disruption of Vision:* Failing to pass on the baton can disrupt the continuity of the family's vision and purpose. Without clear guidance and direction from previous generations, future family members may struggle to uphold the values and principles that define the family's identity.

93

3. Loss of Legacy: Each generation contributes to the family's legacy, but without proper planning and execution in passing on the baton, this legacy may be lost or diluted over time. Important traditions, values, and cultural heritage may fade away, leaving future generations disconnected from their roots.

4. Missed Opportunities for Growth: Effective passing of the baton involves imparting wisdom, sharing experiences, and providing mentorship to younger family members. Without this guidance, younger generations may miss out on valuable opportunities for personal and professional growth, stunting their development and potential.

5. Financial Instability: Inadequate planning for passing on the baton can result in financial instability for the family. Without proper succession planning, assets may be mismanaged or distributed unfairly, leading to financial strain and uncertainty for future generations.

6. Emotional Turmoil: The failure to pass on the baton can create emotional turmoil within the family, causing feelings of resentment, betrayal, or abandonment among family members. This emotional strain can further erode trust and unity within the family, making it difficult to reconcile differences and move forward together.

Overall, the consequences of not passing the baton effectively within the family can have far-reaching implications, affecting not only the present generation but also future generations to come. It underscores the importance of proactive planning, open communication, and a commitment to fostering unity and continuity within the family unit.

Conclusion

As we reach the final pages of "The Neglected Wisdom," I hope you've found this journey to be as thrilling and captivating as I intended it to be. With each turn of the page, you've been presented with wisdom that is ever present yet neglected, simple yet profound, guiding you towards a path of empowerment and self-discovery.

In this book, we've delved deep into the impact of wisdom on our lives, uncovering insights that have the potential to transform our lives. As you close this book, I invite you to reflect on the following key takeaways:

1. Life is a relay race, where each generation passes the baton to the next, ensuring continuity and growth.

2. Reflect on your journey, acknowledging both triumphs and failures, and prepare for the handover to the next runner.

3. Understand how the laws and principles for longevity and vibrant health shape your physical and emotional well-being.

4. Apply the "Neglected Wisdom" to lead a life of harmony, health, and vitality.

5. Embrace life as a multifaceted journey encompassing the physical and spiritual realms.

6. Recognise the disruptive nature of strife within families and organisations, and strive to resolve conflicts with understanding and compassion.

7. Be vigilant against unchecked strife, as it has the potential to fracture relationships, undermine trust, and hinder progress.

8. Draw wisdom from the giants of the past, whose footsteps have left indelible marks on the sands of time.

9. Remember that wisdom is readily available to those who seek it, ask for it, and knock on its door.

As you navigate the complexities of life, may the wisdom gleaned from these pages serve as a guiding light, illuminating your path and empowering you to live a life filled with purpose, joy, and fulfilment. Thank you for accompanying me on this journey, and may the lessons learned within these pages stay with you long after you've turned the final page.

Afterword

As I sat down to reflect on the journey of writing this book, I'm struck by the unexpected turns it has taken and the profound insights it has brought to light. It's surreal to think that I've reached this point, that the words I once scribbled in notebooks and typed into digital documents have coalesced into a cohesive narrative, ready to be shared with the world.

The genesis of this book stretches back to my days as a amazed undergraduate, where I first began to document my thoughts and experiences. Back then, writing was simply a means of self-expression, a way to make sense of the world around me. Little did I know that those early musings would evolve into something much greater.

In 2020, I embarked on the journey of writing this book in earnest, only to set it aside for a time. Life intervened, as it so often does, pulling me in different directions and presenting new challenges. Yet, the seed had been planted, and the ideas continued to simmer beneath the surface.

It wasn't until later, as I reflected on the events of my life and the lessons I had learned along the way, that the vision for this book began to take shape. I found myself drawn to the concept of wisdom, of paying attention to the lessons that life so often tries to impart. As it is written in the Bible - "Wisdom is the principal thing," and in all honesty, it is the principal thing.

As I reflect further on this journey, I'm reminded of a recurring conversation I used to have with myself. I often contemplated what it would be like to face the Almighty and question the mysteries of existence. In those moments of introspection, I imagined God gently reminding us that we have overlooked the wisdom that surrounds us. Too often, we find ourselves repeating the same mistakes, perpetuating events that cause pain and suffering when they could have been avoided. It's a sobering thought, and one that underscores the importance of paying heed to the lessons that life presents us with.

So, I delved into the task of distilling my accumulated wisdom(Wisdom of Chuks with some grey hairs) into these pages, drawing from my own experiences and observations, as well as the insights of others.

In the end, what emerged was more than just a book—it was a testament to the power of listening, of paying attention to the wisdom that surrounds us. It's easy to get caught up in the hustle and bustle of life, to overlook the subtle lessons that are waiting to be learned. But if we take the time to listen—to really listen—we may find that the answers we seek are closer than we think.

As I close this chapter of my journey, I am filled with gratitude—for the opportunity to share my thoughts, insights, and experiences with you, the reader who will embark on this journey, and the wisdom that has guided me along the way. May this book serve as a reminder that wisdom is not just something to be sought after, but something to be embraced, cherished, and shared with others.

Thank you. I love you, dear reader, and please gift and share this book with someone else. Don't forget to kindly leave me a review on Amazon website or any other website you purchased the book from if you can.

Chuks Eze